RICE

DISHES

60 easy recipes
for making good food fast

CHANCELLOR
PRESS

First published in Great Britain by Hamlyn
This edition published in 1996 by Chancellor Press
an imprint of Reed Consumer Books Limited,
Michelin House, 81 Fulham Road, London SW3 6RB

ISBN 1 85153 001 0

A CIP catalogue record for this book
is available from the British Library

ACKNOWLEDGEMENTS
Designed and produced by: The Bridgewater Book Company
Series Editors: Veronica Sperling and Christine McFadden
Art Director: Peter Bridgewater
Designer: Terry Jeavons
Photography: Trevor Wood
Food preparation and styling: Jonathan Higgins
Cookery contributor: Christine McFadden

Produced by Mandarin Offset
Printed and bound in Singapore

NOTES

❧ Standard level spoon measurements are used in all recipes.

❧ Both imperial and metric measurements have been given in all recipes. Use one set of measurements only and not a mixture of both.

❧ Eggs should be size 3 unless otherwise stated.

❧ Milk should be full fat unless otherwise stated.

❧ Fresh herbs should be used unless otherwise stated. If unavailable use dried herbs as an alternative but halve the quantites stated.

❧ Ovens should be preheated to the specified temperature - if using a fan assisted oven, follow manufacturer's instructions for adjusting the time and the temperature.

❧ All microwave information is based on a 650 watt oven. Follow manufacturer's instructions for an oven with a different wattage.

Contents

Introduction

Despite the mystique and ritual surrounding the cooking of rice, it is one of the most versatile and straightforward of grains to prepare. However, the subject is more complex when it comes to defining and recognizing the different varieties of rice. There are thought to be some 10,000 different types, though probably under 10 varieties are available in the West.

LONG-GRAIN: The most popular and versatile rice, used in countless dishes the world over. The grains are slim and about five time longer than they are wide. When cooked, the rice is fluffy, light and dry. Both white and brown are available, as well as 'easy-cook' versions.

MEDIUM-GRAIN: The grain is shorter and wider than the long-grain variety. While absorbing more liquid than long-grain, the grains still remain separate when cooked, although they are soft. The rice can therefore be used for moulded dishes, risottos and puddings.

SHORT-GRAIN: These grains absorb the most liquid of all, and cook to a creamy mass. The rice is really only suitable for puddings. If used in savoury dishes, it should be fried first, and then baked.

BASMATI: Described as the 'prince of rice', this very slender, long-grain rice is prized for its fragrance and nutty taste. It is used in Indian dishes such as biryanis and pilafs. Brown, white, and 'easy-cook' versions are available.

RISOTTO RICE: This is a short-grain white rice from northern Italy. One of the most absorbent of rices, it releases starch during cooking which gives it the characteristic creamy texture of the dish after which it is named. Although creamy, the cooked grains are still firm to the bite. The best known risotto rice is Arborio, but the very best brands are Vialone Nano and Carnaroli.

THAI FRAGRANT (JASMINE RICE): This an aromatic long-grain rice, with a slightly less pronounced flavour than that of basmati rice. Unlike other long-grain rice, it has a soft, slightly sticky texture when cooked. It is suitable for Chinese and Southeast-Asian dishes.

WILD RICE: This is not a rice at all, but the seed from a wild aquatic grass, native to the United States and Canada. The grains are very long and slim, and dark brown in colour. Wild rice is expensive, but it can be made to go further by mixing it with other rice after cooking.

Cooking Perfect Rice

When working out quantities, remember that rice triples in size when cooked. It is hard to specify accurately a single serving size, but in general 50 g/2 oz is plenty for a main meal, with slightly less for a salad.

Opinion is divided on whether or not rice needs washing before cooking. With modern milling and packaging it may not be necessary, but it is recommended for Asian imported rice.

The exact amount of cooking liquid depends on the type and age of the rice, the cooking method, and personal preference. For cooking white long-grain rice by the absorption method, a rough guide is to use one-and-a-half times the volume of liquid to rice. Brown rice will need double the volume of liquid. Reduce or increase the liquid if you prefer firmer or softer rice.

Boiling the rice in plenty of salted water is a useful and foolproof technique. The method keeps the grains separate and saves accurate measuring of liquid.

Absorption Method

SERVES 4

225 g/8 oz white or brown long-grain, or basmati rice	350–450 ml/12-16 fl oz water or stock salt

*P*UT the rice, liquid and salt in a saucepan. Bring to the boil, and stir once.

❦ Cover tightly and simmer over a very low heat for 15–45 minutes, until all the liquid has been absorbed.

Boiling Method

SERVES 4

2 litres/3½ pints water 1 tbsp salt	225 g/8 oz white or brown long-grain, or basmati rice

*B*RING the water to the boil in a large saucepan. Stir in the salt. Gradually add the rice so that the water does not stop boiling. Cook for 10–45 minutes, until tender, testing by biting a grain.

❦ Drain at once, transfer to a warm serving dish, and fluff with a fork. Gently stir in a knob of butter if wished.

Stir-Fried Beef with Golden Rice

SERVES 4

2 tbsp soy sauce
4 tsp cornflour
salt
450 g/1 lb fillet of beef, cut into thin
   1 cm/$\frac{1}{2}$ inch strips
225 g/8 oz long-grain rice
1 tsp turmeric

2 tbsp vegetable oil
1 garlic clove, finely chopped
1 cm/$\frac{1}{2}$ inch piece fresh ginger root,
   finely chopped
300 ml/$\frac{1}{2}$ pint chicken stock
2 tbsp dry sherry
8 spring onions, thinly sliced

*M*IX together 1 tablespoon of the soy sauce, 1 teaspoon of the cornflour and a pinch of salt. Add the beef, and leave for 2 hours to marinate.

❧ Meanwhile, boil the rice with the turmeric in plenty of salted water until tender. Drain and keep warm.

❧ Heat the oil, and stir-fry the garlic and ginger for 1 minute. Add the stock, sherry and remaining soy sauce. Bring to the boil, lower the heat and simmer for 10 minutes.

❧ Mix the remaining cornflour to a paste with a little water.

❧ Increase the heat, and add the beef and spring onions. Stir-fry for 3 minutes. Add the cornflour, and stir-fry for 1–2 minutes, until thickened. Serve at once with the rice.

Creamed Veal and Mushrooms

SERVES 4

25 g/1 oz butter
2 tbsp vegetable oil
700 g/1$\frac{1}{2}$ lb veal fillet, thinly sliced
225 g/8 oz long-grain rice
2 onions, finely chopped

225 g/8 oz mushrooms, thinly sliced
salt and freshly ground black pepper
150 ml/$\frac{1}{4}$ pint double cream
4 tbsp finely chopped fresh parsley
4 tbsp finely chopped fresh mint

*H*EAT the butter and oil in a frying pan until foaming. Add the veal, and sear on all sides. Remove from the pan and set aside.

❧ Boil the rice in plenty of salted water until tender. Drain and keep warm.

❧ Meanwhile, add the onion to the pan, and gently fry for 7 minutes. Add the mushrooms and fry for 2 minutes more.

❧ Return the veal to the pan, season to taste and gently fry for 2–3 minutes. Stir in the cream and herbs, and reheat gently.

❧ Transfer to a serving dish, and serve at once with the rice.

Stir-Fried Pork

SERVES 4

2 tbsp soy sauce
1 tbsp cornflour
225 g/8 oz pork fillet, cut into very
    thin strips
225 g/8 oz long-grain rice

4 tbsp vegetable oil
225 g/8 oz French beans, sliced
1/2 tsp salt
1 tbsp dry sherry
2 tbsp stock

*M*IX together the soy sauce and cornflour. Add the pork, and leave to marinate for about 10 minutes.

❦ Boil the rice in plenty of salted water until tender. Drain and keep warm.

❦ Heat half the oil in a wok, and stir-fry the pork for about 1 minute until lightly coloured. Remove from the pan.

❦ Heat the remaining oil, and stir-fry the beans with the salt for about 1 minute. Stir in the pork, sherry and stock. Stir-fry for another minute until thickened. Serve hot with the rice.

Madras Meat Curry

SERVES 4

2 cardamoms, crushed
1 tbsp coriander seeds, crushed
1 tbsp ground cumin
1 tbsp ground turmeric
1 tsp chilli powder
2 garlic cloves, crushed
450 g/1 lb lean lamb or beef, cut into
    2.5 cm/1 inch cubes

2 tbsp vegetable oil
2 onions, thinly sliced
600 ml/1 pint stock
2 bay leaves
salt and freshly ground black pepper
225 g/8 oz basmati rice
juice of 1/2 lemon

*M*IX together the spices and the garlic. Rub the spice mixture into the meat.

❦ Heat the oil, and fry the onions until golden brown. Remove from the pan and set aside. Add the meat to the pan, and fry until well browned.

❦ Return the onions to the pan with the stock and bay leaves. Bring to the boil, then season to taste, cover and simmer over a low heat for about 1 1/4 hours, until the meat is tender. Add a little more stock if the mixture seems dry.

❦ Meanwhile, boil the rice in plenty of salted water until tender. Drain and keep warm.

❦ Remove the bay leaves from the curry, and stir in the lemon juice. Serve immediately with the rice.

Lamb, Rice and Lentil Pilaf

SERVES 6

4 tbsp vegetable oil
2 onions, very finely chopped
2 garlic cloves, finely chopped
2.5 cm/1 inch piece fresh ginger root
  finely chopped
1 tsp ground cinnamon
seeds from 4 cardamom pods
750 g/1 lb 10 oz boneless lamb, cubed

700 ml/1¼ pint stock
1½ tsp salt
225 g/8 oz basmati rice
100 g/4 oz brown or green lentils
50 g/2 oz raisins
50g/2 oz flaked almonds, toasted
coriander leaves, to garnish

*H*EAT half the oil in a saucepan and fry half each of the onion, garlic and spices for 5 minutes. Add the lamb and fry until brown. Add 150 ml/¼ pint of the stock and ½ teaspoon of the salt. Cover and simmer for 40 minutes.

❧ Meanwhile, heat the remaining oil, and fry the remaining onion and spices until the onion is golden.

❧ Stir in the rice, lentils, raisins and remaining salt.

❧ Add the remaining stock and bring to the boil. Cover and simmer for 20 minutes, then leave to stand for 10 minutes.

❧ Transfer to a warm dish, and stir in the almonds. Add the lamb, with some of the broth and garnish with coriander.

Mexican Beef with Lime Rice

SERVES 4

450 g/1 lb lean minced beef
2 tbsp vegetable oil
1 onion, finely chopped
1 green or red pepper, diced
2 garlic cloves, chopped finely
1 tbsp tomato purée
½ tsp chilli powder, or to taste
1 tsp cumin seeds, toasted

150 g/5 oz frozen sweetcorn kernels
225 g/8 oz cooked kidney beans
450 ml/16 fl oz stock
salt and freshly ground black pepper
225 g/8 oz long-grain rice
300 ml/½ pint water
juice of 2 limes
3 tbsp finely chopped fresh coriander

*F*RY the beef in the oil until no longer pink. Add the onion, pepper and garlic, and fry until just soft.

❧ Add the tomato purée, chilli powder, cumin, sweetcorn, beans and stock. Season to taste. Bring to the boil, then simmer for 45 minutes, stirring occasionally.

❧ Put the rice, water, lime juice and ½ teaspoon of salt in a saucepan. Bring to the boil and stir once. Cover and simmer for 15 minutes. Fluff with a fork and stir in the coriander. Serve with the beef.

Pork and Roasted Pepper Sauce

SERVES 6

350 g/12 oz long-grain brown rice	1 tbsp wine vinegar
2 each red and yellow peppers	300 ml/½ pint stock
1 small onion, finely chopped	25 g/1 oz butter
3 garlic cloves, finely chopped	salt and freshly ground black pepper
3 tbsp olive oil	800 g/1¾ lb pork fillet, thinly sliced
2 tbsp tomato purée	chopped fresh parsley, to garnish

$\mathcal{B}$OIL the rice in plenty of salted water for about 30 minutes, until tender. Drain and keep warm.

❧ Grill the peppers for about 10 minutes, turning frequently, until the skins begin to blacken. Remove the skins and seeds, and chop the flesh.

❧ Gently fry the onion and garlic in 1 tablespoon of the oil. Add the tomato purée, vinegar and stock. Simmer for 5 minutes.

❧ Purée in a blender with the peppers, push through a sieve, and return to the pan. Whisk in the butter and season to taste.

❧ Heat the remaining oil, and stir-fry the pork until brown. Season to taste. Stir in the sauce, simmer for 1–2 minutes. Garnish with parsley, and serve with the rice.

Dry Lamb Curry with Ginger

SERVES 4

1 tbsp vegetable oil	2.5 cm/1 inch piece fresh ginger root
1 onion, chopped	finely chopped
1 tbsp curry powder	salt and freshly ground black pepper
450 g/1 lb lean lamb, cubed	225 g/8 oz long-grain rice
2 tsp vinegar	300 ml/½ pint water
1 tbsp tomato purée	1 tbsp desiccated coconut

$\mathcal{H}$EAT the oil, and fry the onion until golden. Stir in the curry powder, and cook gently for 2 minutes. Add the lamb, and brown lightly.

❧ Stir in the vinegar, tomato purée and ginger and season to taste. Stir well, bring to the boil and cover. Simmer gently, stirring occasionally, for about 1 hour, until the meat is tender. Add a little water if the mixture becomes too dry.

❧ About 20 minutes before serving, put the rice, water and ½ teaspoon salt in a saucepan. Bring to the boil and stir once. Cover and simmer for 15 minutes or until the rice is tender and all the liquid has been absorbed.

❧ Stir the coconut into the curry, and serve with the rice.

Pork and Apricot Casserole

SERVES 6

800 g/1¾ lb lean pork, cut into
    2.5 x 1 cm/1 x ½ inch slices
2 tbsp seasoned flour
1 tsp dried thyme
4 tbsp olive oil
2 onions, sliced
1 garlic clove, crushed
4 celery stalks, thinly sliced

300 ml/½ pint chicken stock
225 g/8 oz dried apricots, soaked
    in 300 ml/½ pint orange juice
salt and freshly ground black pepper
225 g/8 oz long-grain rice
2 tsp finely chopped fresh parsley,
    to garnish

*T*oss the pork in the flour and thyme. Heat the oil in a casserole, and gently fry the pork for 5 minutes.

❦ Add the onions, garlic and celery, and gently fry for about 4 minutes.

❦ Stir in the chicken stock with the apricots and their soaking liquid. Season to taste and bring to the boil.

❦ Cook in a preheated oven at 180°C/350°F/gas mark 4 for 45 minutes until the pork and vegetables are tender.

❦ Meanwhile, boil the rice in plenty of salted water until tender. Drain and keep warm.

❦ Garnish the pork with the parsley, and serve with the rice.

Cantonese Barbecued Pork

SERVES 6

3 tbsp dry sherry
2 tbsp light soy sauce
1 tbsp dark soy sauce
2 tbsp hoisin sauce

1 kg/2¼ lb pork fillet, cut lengthways
    into thin strips
350 g/12 oz Thai fragrant rice
3 tbsp clear honey

*M*ix together the sherry, soy sauces, and hoisin sauce. Add the pork strips and leave to marinate for about 45 minutes.

❦ Drain the pork, and arrange the strips on a rack. Roast in a preheated oven at 200°C/400°F/gas mark 6 for 30 minutes. Place a dish of water below the pork to catch the fat.

❦ Meanwhile, boil the rice in plenty of salted water until tender. Drain and keep warm.

❦ Remove the pork from the oven, and allow to cool for about 3 minutes. Brush with the honey, then roast for a further 2 minutes. Serve immediately with the rice.

Spicy Beef and Aubergine Rice

SERVES 4–6

225 g/8 oz Thai fragrant rice
3–4 tbsp groundnut oil
1 tsp coriander seeds
2 garlic cloves, finely chopped
½ tsp finely chopped fresh ginger
root
¼–½ tsp dried red chilli flakes

700g/1½ lb sirloin steak, thinly
sliced
1 large aubergine, cubed
1 tbsp soy sauce
2–3 tbsp stock
salt and freshly ground black pepper

*B*OIL the rice in plenty of salted water for 10–12 minutes until tender. Drain well and keep warm.

❧ Heat the oil in a wok until almost smoking. Stir-fry the coriander, garlic, ginger and chilli for a few seconds. Add the beef and stir-fry until just browned. Remove from the pan.

❧ Add the aubergine, and stir-fry for about 5 minutes, until beginning to colour, adding a little more oil if necessary.

❧ Return the beef to the pan, stir in the soy sauce and stock. Season to taste and stir for 1 minute. Serve with the rice.

Paprika Beef with Rice

SERVES 4

2 tbsp vegetable oil
50 g/2 oz butter
1 onion, thinly sliced
1 garlic clove, crushed
2 celery stalks, thinly sliced
450 g/1 lb minced beef
1 tbsp flour
1 tbsp paprika

1 bay leaf
300 ml/½ pint beef stock
salt and freshly ground black pepper
225 g/8 oz long-grain rice
100 g/4 oz button mushrooms, sliced
3 tbsp soured cream
1 tbsp finely chopped fresh parsley,
to garnish

*H*EAT the oil and half the butter, and gently fry the onion, garlic and celery for 4 minutes, stirring occasionally. Add the beef, and fry until evenly browned. Stir in the flour and paprika, and fry for 2 minutes more.

❧ Add the bay leaf and stock, season to taste, and bring to the boil. Cover and simmer gently for about 50 minutes.

❧ Boil the rice in plenty of salted water until tender, then drain.

❧ Fry the mushrooms in the remaining butter for 5 minutes.

❧ Remove the bay leaf from the meat, stir in the soured cream and heat gently. Transfer the meat to a serving dish, and surround it with the rice. Top with the mushrooms, and garnish with the parsley.

Lamb Casserole
with Roasted Garlic and Chilli

SERVES 4

2 large fresh chillies	100 g/4 oz cooked chick-peas
2 large garlic cloves, unpeeled	400 g/14 oz can chopped tomatoes
1 tsp each coriander and cumin seeds, toasted and crushed	1 large aubergine, cubed
700 g/1½ lb boneless lamb, cubed	75 g/3 oz green beans, chopped
3 tbsp vegetable oil	425 ml/¾ pint stock
1 onion, chopped	salt and freshly ground black pepper
350 g/12 oz cooked brown long-grain rice	3 tbsp chopped fresh coriander
	plain yogurt, to serve

*R*OAST the chillies and garlic in a preheated oven at 220°C/425°F/gas mark 7 for 15–20 minutes. Remove the skins and seeds from the chilli and the skins from the garlic. Mash to a paste with the coriander and cumin seeds.

❧ Brown the lamb in 1 tablespoon of the oil, and set aside.

❧ Heat the remaining oil and gently fry the onion for 5 minutes. Add the chilli paste and stir-fry for another minute.

❧ Add the lamb, together with the rice, chick-peas, tomatoes, aubergine, beans, stock and seasoning. Bring to the boil, then cover and simmer gently for 1–1½ hours, until tender. Stir in the coriander, and serve with yogurt.

Chilli con Carne

SERVES 4

2 tbsp vegetable oil	½–1 tsp chilli powder
3 onions, chopped	450 g/16 oz cooked kidney beans
1 red pepper, seeded and diced	400 g/14 oz can chopped tomatoes
2 garlic cloves, crushed	½ tsp ground cumin
450 g/1 lb lean minced beef	salt and freshly ground black pepper
450 ml/16 fl oz beef stock	225 g/8 oz long-grain rice

*H*EAT the oil in a pan, add the onions, red pepper and garlic and gently fry until soft. Add the meat and fry until just coloured. Blend in the stock, and add the chilli powder, beans, tomatoes and cumin. Season to taste.

❧ Bring to the boil, then cover and simmer over a low heat for 50–60 minutes, stirring occasionally.

❧ Boil the rice in plenty of salted water until tender. Drain and serve with the chilli.

Chicken Suprême

SERVES 4

25 g/1 oz butter	225 g/8 oz long-grain rice
100 g/4 oz mushrooms, thinly sliced	2 tsp lemon juice
1 small onion, chopped	350 g/12 oz cooked chicken, sliced
1 tbsp finely chopped fresh parsley	1 egg yolk, beaten
25 g/1 oz flour	4 tbsp double cream
300 ml/½ pint chicken stock	salt and freshly ground black pepper

*M*ELT the butter in a saucepan, and gently fry the mushrooms, onion and 1 tablespoon of the parsley for 5 minutes. Stir in the flour, and cook for 1 minute. Gradually stir in the stock, and bring to the boil, stirring constantly. Lower the heat, cover and simmer gently for 20–30 minutes.

❧ Boil the rice in plenty of salted water until tender, then drain and keep warm.

❧ Strain the sauce if wished, and stir in the lemon juice. Add the chicken to the sauce, and heat through for about 5 minutes.

❧ Combine the egg yolk and cream, season and stir in 3 tablespoons of the hot sauce. Add to the pan and heat gently.

❧ Arrange the rice around the edge of a serving dish, with the chicken and sauce into the centre.

Chinese Chicken with Peppers

SERVES 4

225 g/ 8 oz long-grain rice	2 slices fresh ginger root, finely chopped
225 g/8 oz boneless, skinless chicken breasts, chopped	2 spring onions, shredded
½ tsp salt	2 fresh chillies, seeded and chopped
1 egg white	1 red pepper, seeded and diced
1 tbsp cornflour	1 green pepper, seeded and diced
4 tbsp vegetable oil	2 tbsp black bean sauce

*B*OIL the rice in plenty of salted water until tender. Drain and keep warm.

❧ Mix the chicken with the salt, egg white and cornflour.

❧ Heat the oil in a wok, and stir-fry the chicken until lightly coloured. Remove from the pan.

❧ Raise the heat and stir-fry the ginger, spring onions and chillies for a few seconds, then add the peppers. Stir-fry for 30 seconds, then add the black bean sauce and the chicken. Stir-fry for 1 minute. Serve immediately with the rice.

Turkey Stroganoff with Green Peppercorns

SERVES 4

225 g/8 oz long-grain rice
700 g/1½ lb turkey escalopes,
   cut into thin strips
1 tbsp green peppercorns
seasoned flour, for dusting
3 tbsp vegetable oil

1 onion, thinly sliced
225 g/8 oz mushrooms, sliced
salt
300 ml/½ pint soured cream
finely grated zest of ½ lemon
paprika, to garnish

*B*OIL the rice in plenty of salted water until tender. Drain well and keep warm.

❧ Rub the turkey with the peppercorns, dust with flour, then fry in half the oil until golden. Remove from the pan.

❧ Gently fry the onion and mushrooms in the remaining oil for 5 minutes, until soft.

❧ Return the turkey to the pan and season to taste. Stir in the soured cream and lemon zest, and warm through gently.

❧ Serve on top of the rice, garnished with a dusting of paprika.

Duck and Brazil Nut Pilaf

SERVES 4–6

1 tbsp olive oil
1 small onion, finely chopped
225 g/8 oz easy-cook mixed
   long-grain and wild rice
450 ml/16 fl oz chicken stock
250 g/9 oz cooked duck breast,
   chopped
½ green pepper, seeded and diced

50 g/2 oz shelled Brazil nuts, toasted
   and roughly chopped
50g/2 oz dried apricots, chopped
1 tbsp finely grated orange zest
salt and freshly ground black pepper
2 tbsp coarsely chopped fresh flat-
   leafed parsley

*H*EAT the oil in a large saucepan and gently fry the onion until golden.

❧ Stir in the rice, fry for 1–2 minutes, then add the stock. Bring to the boil and simmer for 5 minutes.

❧ Add the duck, pepper, Brazil nuts, apricots and orange zest. Season to taste, then simmer for 15 minutes until all the stock has been absorbed.

❧ Transfer to a warm serving dish, and garnish with parsley.

VARIATION: For Duck, Fennel and Hazelnut Pilaf, use one fennel bulb instead of the onion, and toasted hazelnuts instead of the Brazil nuts.

Coronation Chicken

SERVES 8–10

2 x 1.5 kg/3 lb chickens
salt and freshly ground black pepper
1 carrot, quartered
1 celery stalk, roughly chopped
bouquet garni
450 g/1 lb long-grain rice
100 g/4 oz flaked almonds, toasted
    to garnish
fresh coriander, to garnish

SAUCE:
2 onions, finely chopped
3 tbsp vegetable oil
2 tbsp hot or mild curry powder
300 ml/½ pint dry white wine
8 canned apricot halves, puréed
600 ml/1 pint mayonnaise
juice of 1 large lemon
150 ml/¼ pint whipping cream
    whipped

*P*LACE the chickens in a saucepan with just enough water to cover. Season, and add the carrot, celery and bouquet garni. Bring to the boil, cover and simmer for 1 hour.

❧ Cool the chicken in the cooking liquid. Lift out and remove the meat from the bones.

❧ Reserve 150 ml/¼ pint of stock for the sauce. Bring 600 ml/1 pint of the remaining stock to the boil. Add the rice, cover and simmer until tender. Allow the rice to cool.

❧ Fry the onion in the oil with the curry powder, until soft. Add the wine and reserved stock, and season to taste. Simmer for 10 minutes. Purée until smooth, strain and allow to cool.

❧ Stir in the apricots, mayonnaise, lemon juice, cream and chicken. Arrange the rice on a serving dish, and top with the chicken mixture. Garnish with the almonds and coriander.

Chicken and Avocado Rice Salad

SERVES 4

350 g/12 oz cooked long-grain rice
200 g/7 oz cooked or canned red
    kidney beans, drained
2 large spring onions, green parts
    included, sliced diagonally
175 g/6 oz cooked chicken, diced
1 large ripe avocado, chopped
mint sprigs, to garnish

LEMON MINT DRESSING:
finely grated zest and juice of
    1 lemon
pinch of cayenne pepper
1 garlic clove, finely chopped
2 tsp finely chopped fresh mint
¼ tsp salt
6 tbsp extra virgin olive oil

*W*HISK the dressing ingredients until thick. Mix the rice, beans and spring onions in a serving dish. Stir in half the dressing and leave to stand for 1 hour.

❧ Arrange the chicken and avocado on top. Pour over the remaining dressing, garnish with mint, and serve immediately.

Chicken Pilaf

SERVES 4

25 g/1 oz butter
1 onion, chopped
225 g/8 oz basmati rice
salt and freshly ground black pepper
1 bay leaf

400 ml/14 fl oz boiling chicken stock
50 g/2 oz sultanas
25 g/1 oz almonds, toasted and
  chopped
350 g/12 oz cooked chicken, cut into
  bite-size pieces

*M*ELT the butter in a large saucepan, and gently fry the onion for 5 minutes until soft.

❦ Stir in the rice, seasoning and the bay leaf. Add the stock, cover and simmer gently for 20 minutes until all the liquid has been absorbed.

❦ Add the sultanas, almonds and chicken and cook gently, uncovered, for a further 5 minutes until thoroughly heated.

❦ Transfer to a warm serving dish and serve immediately.

Dry Chicken Curry with Yellow Rice

SERVES 4

50 g/2 oz butter
1 onion, chopped
1 garlic clove, crushed
2 tsp curry powder
2 tsp salt
1 tsp chilli powder
1.1 kg/2½ lb chicken, jointed
150 ml/¼ pint water
400 g/14 oz can chopped tomatoes
2 tbsp plain yogurt

YELLOW RICE:
25 g/1 oz butter
225 g/8 oz basmati rice
1 tsp turmeric
1 tsp ground cloves
1 tsp ground cumin
½ tsp salt
600 ml/1 pint boiling water
small piece cucumber, cut into strips

*M*ELT the butter in a large pan, and gently fry the onion and garlic until golden. Add the curry powder, salt, chilli powder and chicken. Fry, stirring occasionally, until the chicken is brown all over. Add the water, cover and simmer over a low heat for 45 minutes, stirring occasionally .

❦ Add the tomatoes and yogurt to the chicken and simmer for a further 5 minutes.

❦ About 15 minutes before serving, melt the butter in a large pan, and fry the rice until translucent. Stir in the turmeric, cloves, cumin and salt, and add the boiling water. Cover and simmer for 15 minutes, until the liquid has been absorbed.

❦ Add the cucumber strips to the rice, and serve with the curry.

Turkey à la King

SERVES 4

1 small onion, finely chopped
75 g/3 oz button mushrooms
2 tbsp vegetable oil
25 g/1 oz flour
300 ml/½ pint milk
150 ml/¼ pint turkey stock
450 g/1 lb cooked turkey meat, diced
100 g/4 oz frozen sweetcorn kernels

3 tbsp double cream
salt and freshly ground black pepper
225 g/8 oz long-grain rice
300 ml/½ pint water
1 red pepper, finely chopped,
   to garnish
1 tbsp finely chopped fresh parsley,
   to garnish

GENTLY fry the onion and mushrooms in the oil for 5 minutes. Stir in the flour, then gradually stir in the milk and stock. Bring to the boil and stir until smooth.

❧ Add the diced turkey, sweetcorn and cream, and season to taste. Allow the mixture to stand so the flavours blend together.

❧ Put the rice, water and ½ teaspoon salt in a saucepan. Bring to the boil and stir once. Cover and simmer for 15 minutes or until the rice is tender and all liquid has been absorbed.

❧ Meanwhile, reheat the turkey mixture for 7–8 minutes. Transfer to a serving dish, garnish with the red pepper and parsley, and serve with the rice.

Chicken Korma

SERVES 4

2 large onions, thinly sliced
2 fresh chillies, seeded and chopped
2 tbsp vegetable oil
1 tbsp ground cumin
2 tsp coriander seeds, crushed
½ tsp turmeric
½ tsp ground ginger
½ tsp ground fenugreek

700 g/1½ lb boneless, skinless
   chicken, diced
2 cardamoms, crushed
1 tbsp ground almonds
300 ml/½ pint plain yogurt
salt
225 g/8 oz basmati rice
lemon wedges, to garnish

FRY the onions and chillies in the oil until the onions are brown. Add the spices, except the cardamoms. Continue to fry until the spices darken in colour.

❧ Add the chicken, cardamoms, ground almonds, half the yogurt and salt to taste. Simmer until the chicken is cooked, adding a little water if necessary.

❧ Boil the rice in plenty of salted water until tender, then drain.

❧ Stir the remaining yogurt into the chicken mixture, garnish with the lemon wedges and serve with the rice.

Duck Breast, Mangetout and Rice Salad

SERVES 4–6

4 boneless duck breasts
salt and freshly ground black pepper
100 g/4 oz mangetout, trimmed
450 g/1 lb cooked long-grain rice
3 spring onions, green parts included,
    finely sliced
3 tbsp finely chopped fresh coriander
40 g/1½ oz unsalted peanuts, toasted

DRESSING:
6 tbsp extra virgin olive oil
juice of 2 limes
1 tsp balsamic vinegar
1 garlic clove, finely chopped
1 tsp ground cumin
salt and freshly ground black pepper

*P*RICK the duck skin, season, and place skin side down in a grill pan. Grill under a medium heat for 10 minutes. Turn over and grill for a further 15 minutes, increasing the heat to crisp the skin. Allow to cool, then slice thinly.

❦ Plunge the mangetout into boiling water for 1 minute. Drain under cold water, and pat dry. Cut the pods in half.

❦ Put the rice in a serving dish, and stir in the mangetout, onion, coriander and peanuts. Arrange the duck on top.

❦ Whisk the dressing ingredients, then pour over the salad.

Chicken and Broccoli Risotto with Chilli

SERVES 4–6

2 boneless, skinless chicken breasts,
    diced
2 tbsp olive oil
40 g/1½ oz butter
½ onion, very finely chopped
1 garlic clove, finely chopped
1-2 fresh red chillies, seeded and
    very finely chopped

250 g/9 oz risotto rice
1 litre/1¾ pints boiling chicken stock,
    kept simmering
225 g/8 oz broccoli florets, stalks
    removed
3 tbsp freshly grated Parmesan
    cheese
salt and freshly ground black pepper

*G*ENTLY fry the chicken in the olive oil and 15 g/½ oz of the butter. When no longer pink, add the onion and fry for 5 minutes until translucent. Add the garlic and chilli, and fry until the garlic is golden.

❦ Add the rice, and stir for a minute or two. Add the hot stock, a ladleful at a time, stirring constantly and allowing the liquid to be absorbed before adding more. The process will take about 25 minutes, leaving the rice creamy but still firm to bite.

❦ Plunge the broccoli florets in boiling water for 1 minute. Drain and add to the rice, together with the Parmesan cheese, salt and pepper, and remaining butter.

Chicken and Celery Stir-Fry

SERVES 4

225 g/8 oz long-grain brown rice
250 g/9 oz boneless, skinless chicken, shredded
½ tsp salt
1 egg white
1 tbsp cornflour
4 tbsp vegetable oil

4 slices fresh ginger root, finely chopped
2 spring onions, finely sliced
1 small celery stalk, finely sliced
1 green pepper, seeded and diced
2 tbsp soy sauce
1 tbsp dry sherry

*B*OIL the rice in plenty of salted water until tender. Drain and keep warm.

❦ Mix the chicken with the salt, egg white and cornflour.

❦ Heat the oil in a wok, and stir-fry the chicken until lightly coloured. Remove from the pan.

❦ Raise the heat and stir-fry the ginger, spring onions, celery and green pepper for 30 seconds. Add the chicken, soy sauce and sherry. Blend well, and stir-fry for a further 1–1½ minutes.

❦ Serve immediately with the rice.

Chicken, Pepper and Aubergine Stir-Fry

SERVES 4

225 g/8 oz Thai fragrant rice
5 tbsp sunflower oil
1 aubergine, peeled and cut into thin 4 cm/1½ inch strips
1 red pepper, seeded and sliced
½ small onion, thinly sliced
2 tsp toasted sesame oil
1 cm/½ inch piece fresh root ginger, finely chopped

3 garlic cloves, finely chopped
1 small fresh red chilli, seeded and finely chopped
250 g/9 oz boneless, skinless chicken, cut into 2 cm/¾ inch pieces
2 tbsp shoyu (Japanese soy sauce)
1 tsp sugar
75 ml/3 fl oz stock
freshly ground black pepper

*B*OIL the rice in plenty of salted water for 10–12 minutes, until tender. Drain well and keep warm.

❦ Meanwhile, heat 4 tablespoons of the oil in a wok until almost smoking. Stir-fry the aubergine, pepper and onion for 3-4 minutes until just coloured. Remove from the pan.

❦ Heat the remaining sunflower oil and the sesame oil. Add the ginger, garlic and chilli, and stir-fry for 10 seconds. Add the chicken and stir-fry for 2 minutes. Return the aubergine mixture to the pan, and stir-fry for 1 minute.

❦ Add the shoyu, sugar and stock, and stir-fry for 2 minutes. Season to taste, and serve with the rice.

Seafood Rice

SERVES 4–6

175 g/6 oz monkfish, cut into chunks
175 g/6 oz sliced squid
6 tbsp olive oil
1 large onion, finely chopped
6 tomatoes, peeled, seeded and chopped
2 tsp paprika
1 large garlic clove, crushed

salt and freshly ground black pepper
350 g/12 oz long-grain rice
900 ml/1½ pints fish or chicken stock
450 ml/¾ pint mussels, scrubbed and bearded
175 g/6 oz peeled prawns
100 g/4 oz lobster or crabmeat, flaked

*F*RY the monkfish and squid in the oil until golden. Add the onion, tomatoes, paprika and garlic, and season to taste. Cook, stirring, for 1–2 minutes.

❧ Add the rice and stock, and bring to the boil. Simmer gently for 5 minutes without stirring.

❧ Place the mussels and prawns on top of the rice and continue cooking for a further 15 minutes.

❧ Discard any mussels that have not opened. Add the lobster or crabmeat, and cook for a further 5 minutes until all the liquid has been absorbed.

❧ Stir the seafood into the rice, and serve immediately.

Swordfish Casserole

SERVES 4

2 red peppers, seeded and chopped
1 onion, chopped
1 tbsp olive oil
1 garlic clove, finely chopped
1 tbsp white wine vinegar
1 tbsp tomato purée
1 tbsp finely chopped fresh thyme
250 ml/9 fl oz fish stock

salt and freshly ground black pepper
225 g/8 oz trimmed celery, sliced
700 g/1½ lb swordfish, cubed
225 g/8 oz long-grain rice
8 sliced, pitted black olives, to garnish
chopped celery leaves, to garnish

*G*ENTLY fry the pepper and onion in the oil until just soft. Add the garlic, vinegar, tomato purée, thyme, and stock. Simmer for 5 minutes then season to taste.

❧ Purée in a blender until smooth, then transfer to a casserole.

❧ Add the celery and swordfish, and bring to the boil. Cover and bake in the oven for 35 minutes.

❧ Meanwhile, boil the rice in plenty of salted water until tender. Drain and keep warm.

❧ Transfer the fish to a serving dish, garnish with the olives and celery leaves, and serve with the rice.

Tuna and Chilli Salad with Lime Dressing

SERVES 4

450 g/1 lb cooked long-grain rice
3 tomatoes, peeled, seeded and diced
1 yellow pepper, seeded and diced
4 spring onions, finely chopped
1 fresh chilli, seeded and chopped
3 tbsp chopped fresh coriander
mixed green salad leaves
200 g/7 oz can tuna fish, drained and flaked

2 hard-boiled eggs, quartered
pitted black olives, to garnish
DRESSING:
juice of 2 limes
1 tsp balsamic vinegar
1 garlic clove, chopped finely
1 tsp ground cumin
salt and freshly ground black pepper
6 tbsp extra virgin olive oil

COMBINE the rice, tomatoes, green pepper, spring onions, chilli and coriander.

❧ Whisk the dressing ingredients until thick. Pour over the rice mixture, and toss lightly.

❧ Place on a bed of salad leaves, and top with the tuna, hard-boiled eggs and olives.

Chillied Fish

SERVES 4

225 g/8 oz long-grain rice
300 ml/½ pint water
½ tsp salt
450 g/1 lb fish fillet e.g. cod or plaice, cut into 5 cm/2 inch slices
flour, for coating
300 ml/½ pint vegetable oil

SAUCE:
2 tsp finely chopped fresh ginger root
1 tbsp chopped spring onion
3 tbsp dry sherry
1 tbsp soy sauce
2 tsp sugar
1 tsp salt
1 tsp vinegar
½–1 tbsp chilli sauce

PUT the rice, water and salt in a saucepan. Bring to the boil and stir once. Cover and simmer for 15 minutes or until the rice is tender and the liquid has been absorbed.

❧ Combine the sauce ingredients, and coat the fish with flour.

❧ Heat the oil in a large frying pan or wok, then fry the fish for 3 minutes. Remove the fish and reheat the oil. Return the fish to the pan to crisp it. Remove and drain.

❧ Pour off all about 1 tablespoon of the oil. Add the sauce to the pan with the fish. Stir well, and simmer for 1 minute. Serve immediately with the rice.

Prawn Curry

SERVES 4

1 onion, chopped	40 g/1½ oz desiccated coconut
2 garlic cloves, crushed	2 tbsp plain yogurt
½ tsp turmeric	300 ml/½ pint water
1 tsp mustard seed	225 g/8 oz long-grain rice
½ tsp chilli powder	450 g/1 lb peeled prawns
½ tsp ground fenugreek	juice of ½ lemon
2 tbsp vegetable oil	salt and freshly ground black pepper

GENTLY fry the onion, garlic and spices in the oil until soft. Stir in the coconut, yogurt and water. Bring to the boil, then simmer for 10 minutes, stirring occasionally.

❧ Meanwhile, boil the rice in plenty of salted water until tender. Drain and keep warm.

❧ Stir the prawns and lemon juice into the onion and spice mixture, and simmer for a further 10 minutes. Season to taste.

❧ Serve immediately with the rice.

Fish Pilaf

SERVES 4–6

2 tsp coriander seeds, toasted and crushed	4 tbsp vegetable oil
2 tsp cumin seeds, toasted and crushed	700 g/1½ lb filleted white fish, cubed
½ tsp turmeric	salt
½ tsp ground fenugreek	2 large onions, finely chopped
1 cm/½ inch piece fresh ginger root, finely chopped	450 g/1 lb basmati rice
	juice of ½ lemon
	coriander leaves, to garnish

MIX together the coriander seeds, cumin, turmeric, fenugreek and ginger. Heat half the oil in a large pan, and fry the spice mixture for about 1 minute.

❧ Add the fish, and pour over just enough water to cover. Season to taste, and simmer for 7–10 minutes until the fish is cooked. Remove with a fish slice and keep warm. Reserve the cooking liquid.

❧ Heat the remaining oil, and fry the onions until brown.

❧ Stir in the rice, then add the reserved fish liquid and lemon juice. Simmer gently until the rice is tender. Add extra water if necessary.

❧ Transfer the rice to a serving dish and arrange the fish on top. Garnish with coriander leaves and serve immediately.

Prawn Risotto

SERVES 4–6

450 g/1 lb unpeeled prawns
1 small fennel bulb, sliced
parsley sprigs
1/2 onion, roughly chopped
1 small carrot, roughly chopped
1 litre/1³/4 pints water
300 ml/1/2 pint dry white wine
100 g/4 oz butter

2 tbsp olive oil
450 g/1 lb risotto rice
salt and freshly ground black pepper
1 garlic clove, crushed
grated zest of 1/2 lemon
fennel leaves, chopped
50 g/2 oz freshly grated Parmesan
cheese

*P*EEL the prawns and reserve the shells. Put the shells, heads and any roe in a pan. Add the fennel, parsley, onion, carrot and water. Simmer gently for 25–30 minutes. Strain and make up to 1.6 litres/2³/4 pints with the white wine and extra water. Bring to the boil and keep simmering.

❧ Heat half the butter and the oil in a pan, and gently fry the rice for 5 minutes. Add a ladleful of the prawn stock, and simmer, stirring, until absorbed. Continue until all the stock has been used up and the rice is tender. Season to taste.

❧ Melt the remaining butter in a small pan, and stir in the prawns, garlic, lemon zest and fennel leaves. Stir into the rice, together with the Parmesan cheese, and serve immediately.

Prawn Fried Rice

SERVES 4

175 g/6 oz long-grain rice
2 spring onions, finely chopped
3 eggs
salt and freshly ground black pepper
4 tbsp vegetable oil

50 g/2 oz prawns, peeled
50 g/2 oz cooked ham, finely diced
100 g/4 oz frozen peas, thawed
1¹/2 tsp soy sauce

*B*OIL the rice in plenty of salted water until tender. Drain and set aside.

❧ Mix half the spring onions with the eggs, season to taste and beat lightly.

❧ Heat one-third of the oil in a wok. Add the eggs and stir until scrambled. Transfer to a warm plate and break up with a fork.

❧ Heat half the remaining oil. Stir-fry the prawns, ham, and peas for 1 minute. Season to taste. Remove from the pan.

❧ Heat the remaining oil, and add the remaining spring onion and the cooked rice. Stir in the soy sauce, then the eggs and the prawn mixture and reheat gently.

Monkfish Pilaf

SERVES 4

700 g/1½ lb monkfish, cubed
175 g/6 oz brown basmati rice
350 ml/12 fl oz stock
100 g/4 oz carrot, grated
100 g/4 oz trimmed spring greens,
  finely sliced
25 g/1 oz walnut halves, chopped

chopped fresh coriander or flat-leafed
  parsley, to garnish
MARINADE:
6 tbsp olive oil
2 tbsp lemon juice
⅛ tsp chilli powder
salt and freshly ground black pepper

*C*OMBINE the marinade ingredients in a bowl. Add the monkfish, then cover and refrigerate for at least 4 hours.
❧ Put the rice, stock and ½ teaspoon salt in a saucepan. Bring to the boil, then cover and simmer for about 40 minutes.
❧ Place the fish in an ovenproof dish under a hot grill for 6–8 minutes, turning and brushing with the marinade.
❧ Steam the vegetables over boiling water for 5 minutes.
❧ Transfer the rice to a serving dish. Stir in the vegetables and walnuts, top with the fish, and sprinkle with coriander.

Paella

SERVES 4–6

3 tbsp olive oil
4 chicken joints
1 large onion, sliced
1 red pepper, seeded and sliced
4 tomatoes, peeled, seeded and
  chopped
1 garlic clove, crushed
225 g/8 oz long-grain rice
¼ tsp powdered saffron

salt and freshly ground black pepper
600 ml/1 pint hot chicken stock
8 mussels, scrubbed and bearded
12 whole prawns, washed and legs
  removed
100 g/4 oz piece garlic sausage,
  chopped
50 g/2 oz frozen peas
lemon wedges, to garnish

*H*EAT 2 tablespoons of the oil and quickly brown the chicken joints. Remove from the pan.
❧ Wipe the pan and heat the remaining oil. Gently fry the onion, pepper, tomatoes and garlic for 8–10 minutes.
❧ Stir in the rice, saffron and seasoning. Cook for 3 minutes, then stir in the stock. Bring the mixture slowly to the boil.
❧ Gently stir with a fork, then arrange the chicken, mussels, prawns, garlic sausage and peas on top of the rice. Cover and simmer for 15–20 minutes until the liquid has been absorbed.
❧ Discard any mussels that have not opened. Garnish with lemon wedges and serve immediately.

Prawn Jambalaya

SERVES 6

4 tbsp olive oil
1 large onion, finely chopped
1 green pepper, seeded and diced
2 celery stalks, finely chopped
3 garlic cloves, finely chopped
350 g/12 oz long-grain rice
2 tsp dried herbes de Provence
1/4 tsp harissa sauce (or 1/2 tsp
  chilli powder)

350 g/12 oz large peeled prawns
225 g/8 oz chorizo sausage, diced
400 g/14 oz can chopped tomatoes
salt and freshly ground black pepper
500 ml/18 fl oz hot stock
3 spring onions, green parts included,
  finely chopped

HEAT the oil in a large casserole, and gently fry the onion, pepper, celery and garlic for 5 minutes.

❧ Add the rice, and gently fry, stirring, for 5 minutes.

❧ Add the herbs, harissa sauce, prawns, chorizo sausage, tomatoes, and salt and pepper.

❧ Stir in the hot stock, bring to the boil. Cover and simmer over a low heat for 20–25 minutes, until the rice is tender.

❧ Sprinkle with the spring onions. Cover and leave to rest for 10 minutes before serving.

Seafood Risotto

SERVES 4

50 g/2 oz butter
1 onion, chopped
1 yellow pepper, seeded and chopped
1 red pepper, seeded and chopped
4 tomatoes, peeled, seeded and
  chopped
350 g/12 oz cod, skinned and cut into
  bite-size pieces

8 scallops, cleaned
salt and freshly ground black pepper
225 g/8 oz medium-grain rice
450 ml/16 fl oz hot stock
1 tbsp finely chopped fresh parsley,
  to garnish
2 tbsp freshly grated Parmesan
  cheese

MELT half the butter, and gently fry the onion, peppers and tomatoes for 1 minute, stirring occasionally.

❧ Add the cod and scallops, and fry for a further 3 minutes. Transfer to a bowl, and season to taste.

❧ Melt the remaining butter in the pan and fry the rice for 3 minutes, stirring. Stir in the stock and 1 teaspoon salt. Bring to the boil, lower the heat and cover. Simmer for 15 minutes until the rice is almost tender and the liquid has been absorbed.

❧ Gently stir in the cod mixture and heat for 2 minutes.

❧ Garnish with parsley, and sprinkle with the Parmesan cheese.

Kedgeree

SERVES 4

225 g/8 oz long-grain brown rice
275 g/10 oz smoked haddock
150–200 ml/5-7 fl oz milk
50 g/2 oz butter
1 onion, chopped
3 hard-boiled eggs, chopped

freshly ground black pepper
2 tbsp double cream
1 tbsp finely chopped fresh parsley,
  to garnish
hard-boiled egg slices, to garnish

*B*OIL the rice in plenty of salted water until tender. Drain well and keep warm.

❧ Put the haddock in a saucepan and add just enough milk to cover. Poach gently for 5–6 minutes, then drain and flake.

❧ Melt the butter, and gently fry the onion for 2–3 minutes until soft. Stir in the fish, chopped eggs and the rice. Season with pepper to taste. Heat gently for 1–2 minutes then remove the pan from the heat and stir in the cream.

❧ Transfer to a warm serving dish, garnish with parsley and slices of hard-boiled egg and serve immediately.

Prawns Newburg

SERVES 4

225 g/8 oz long-grain rice
salt and freshly ground black pepper
50 g/2 oz butter
350 g/12 oz peeled prawns
6 tbsp Madeira or sweet sherry
pinch of paprika

2 egg yolks
150 ml/$\frac{1}{4}$ pint single cream
2 tbsp finely chopped fresh parsley
paprika, to garnish
parsley sprigs, to garnish

*B*OIL the rice is plenty of salted water until just tender. Drain well and keep warm.

❧ Meanwhile, melt the butter in a large saucepan, and gently fry the prawns for 3–4 minutes. Stir in the Madeira or sherry, and cook for a further 3 minutes until reduced. Add the paprika and season to taste.

❧ Beat together the egg yolks and cream, and gradually whisk into the pan. Heat through very gently until thickened but do not allow to boil.

❧ Drain the rice, rinse with boiling water and drain again. Stir in the chopped parsley, and arrange on 4 individual plates.

❧ Spoon over the prawn mixture, garnish with paprika and parsley sprigs and serve immediately.

Two-Rice Salad with Carrot and Orange

SERVES 6

350 g/12 oz each cooked long-grain
   and wild rice
2 carrots, shaved into ribbons
50 g/2 oz pine nuts, toasted
2 tbsp finely chopped fresh thyme
finely grated zest of 1 orange

DRESSING:
2 tbsp orange juice
2 tsp rice vinegar
salt and freshly ground black pepper
6 tbsp extra virgin olive oil
2 cm/¾ inch piece fresh ginger root

$\mathcal{P}$UT the rice in a salad bowl with the remaining ingredients.

❧ To make the dressing, put the orange juice, vinegar, seasoning and oil in a small bowl.

❧ Put the ginger in a garlic press and squeeze the juice into the dressing. Whisk until thick.

❧ Pour the dressing over the salad and toss gently.

Green Rice Salad

SERVES 6

700 g/1½ lb cooked long-grain rice
8 tbsp extra virgin olive oil
2 tbsp white wine vinegar
finely grated zest of 1 lime
salt and freshly ground black pepper
50 g/2 oz shelled pistachio nuts
4 spring onions, green parts included,
   finely chopped

175 g/3 oz cooked peas
50 g/2 oz cooked green beans,
   chopped
3 tbsp chopped fresh coriander
1 tbsp each finely chopped fresh
   rocket, mint and sorrel

$\mathcal{P}$UT the rice in a large bowl. Whisk the oil, vinegar, lime zest and seasoning until thick. Pour the dressing over the rice, tossing gently.

❧ Pour boiling water over the pistachio nuts. Leave to stand for 5 minutes, then slip off the skins.

❧ Mix the nuts, onions, peas, beans and herbs with the rice. Leave to stand for 30 minutes before serving.

Vegetable Curry

SERVES 4

4 potatoes, diced
4 carrots, diced
¼ small turnip, diced
100 g/4 oz shelled peas
100 g/4 oz runner beans, chopped
1 tbsp vegetable oil
1 large onion, finely chopped
2 tsp coriander seeds, crushed
1 tsp turmeric

1 tsp ground ginger
1 tsp chilli powder
½ tsp ground cumin
1 garlic clove, crushed
2 tbsp tomato purée
225 g/8 oz basmati rice
1–2 tsp lemon juice
coriander leaves, to garnish

PARBOIL the potatoes, carrots, turnip, peas and beans together in boiling salted water for 5 minutes. Drain and reserve the cooking liquid.

❧ Heat the oil, and fry the onion with the spices until the onion is golden. Add the garlic. Add the tomato purée and enough of the reserved liquid to make a thick sauce. Lower the heat, cover the pan and simmer gently for 10 minutes.

❧ Boil the rice in plenty of salted water until tender. Drain and keep warm.

❧ Stir the parboiled vegetables into the sauce, and season to taste. Cover and simmer until the vegetables are tender. Add lemon juice to taste.

❧ Garnish with coriander leaves, and serve with the rice.

Spicy Lemon Rice with Cashew Nuts

SERVES 4

1 tbsp yellow mustard seeds
3 tbsp vegetable oil
3 bay leaves
½ tsp ground turmeric
225 g/8 oz basmati rice

finely grated zest of 1 lemon
½ tsp salt
350 ml/12 fl oz water
100 g/4 oz cashew nuts, toasted
plain yogurt, to serve

FRY the mustard seeds in the oil until they start to pop. Add the bay leaves and turmeric, and fry for a few seconds.

❧ Add the rice and stir until coated.

❧ Add the lemon zest, salt and water. Bring to the boil and stir once. Cover and simmer over a low heat for 15–20 minutes, until all the water has been absorbed.

❧ Fluff with a fork, stir in the cashew nuts, and serve with plain yogurt.

Three-Cabbage Medley with Dill

SERVES 4–6

225 g/8 oz long-grain rice
½ tsp salt
1 bay leaf
300 ml/½ pint water
225 g/8 oz each red, white and
    savoy cabbage, thinly sliced
50 g/2 oz butter

2 tsp dill seeds
coarse sea salt and freshly ground
    black pepper
squeeze of lemon juice
3 tbsp coarsely chopped fresh
    flat-leafed parsley

*P*UT the rice, salt and bay leaf in a saucepan with the water. Bring to the boil and stir once. Cover and simmer over a low heat for 15 minutes, until all the liquid has been absorbed.

❦ Meanwhile, place the red cabbage in the bottom of a large steamer basket, with the savoy and white cabbages on top. Cover and steam over boiling water for 5 minutes.

❦ Melt the butter in a small saucepan, and add the dill seeds.

❦ Transfer the rice to a warm, shallow serving dish.

❦ Making sure any liquid from the red cabbage has drained from the steamer basket, pile the cabbage on top of the rice. Season generously with coarse sea salt and freshly ground black pepper. Pour the melted butter over the top, add the parsley, and toss gently to mix the colours. Serve immediately.

Red Cabbage with Rice and Nuts

SERVES 4–6

1 onion, finely chopped
4 tbsp olive oil
25 g/1 oz butter
2 garlic cloves, chopped finely
100 g/4 oz mushrooms, chopped
225 g/8 oz shredded red cabbage
2 tbsp chopped fresh thyme

finely grated zest of ½ lemon
450 g/1 lb cooked brown long-grain
    rice
salt and freshly ground black pepper
3–4 tbsp stock
75 g/3 oz toasted hazelnuts, chopped

*G*ENTLY fry the onion in the oil and butter until translucent. Add the garlic, and fry for 2 minutes more.

❦ Add the mushrooms, shredded cabbage, thyme and lemon zest. Fry for another 7–8 minutes, until the cabbage is tender but still crunchy.

❦ Stir in the rice, season to taste, and moisten with a little stock if the mixture seems dry.

❦ Sprinkle with the hazelnuts, and serve at once.

Broccoli and Water Chestnut Stir-Fry

SERVES 4

225 g/8 oz Thai fragrant rice
1/2 tsp salt
300 ml/1/2 pint water
1 tsp cornflour
2 tbsp shoyu
1 tbsp rice vinegar
175 ml/6 fl oz stock

3 tbsp groundnut oil
4 very thin slices fresh ginger root
350 g/12 oz broccoli florets
salt and freshly ground black pepper
100 g/4 oz water chestnuts, halved
1/2 tbsp sesame seeds, toasted

𝒫UT the rice and salt in a saucepan with the water. Bring to the boil, stir once, then cover and simmer over a very low heat for 15 minutes, until all the liquid has been absorbed.
❦ Meanwhile, combine the cornflour, shoyu, rice vinegar and half the stock.
❦ Heat the oil in a wok until almost smoking. Stir-fry the ginger for 10 seconds. Add the broccoli and stir-fry for 30 seconds.
❦ Add the remaining stock and season to taste. Cover and simmer over a medium heat for about 5 minutes.
❦ Add the water chestnuts, cornflour mixture and sesame seeds, and stir until thickened. Serve with the rice.

Herbed Rice with Butternut Squash

SERVES 4

1 tbsp olive oil
50 g/2 oz butter
1 bay leaf
1 small onion, finely chopped
225 g/8 oz brown basmati rice
4 tbsp chopped fresh mixed herbs

1/2 tsp salt
freshly ground black pepper
450 ml/16 fl oz stock
1 small butternut squash (about
    225 g/8 oz), peeled and diced

𝓗EAT the oil and butter, and gently fry the bay leaf and onion for 3 minutes. Add the rice and stir until coated.
❦ Add the herbs, salt and pepper, and stock. Bring to the boil, then cover and simmer over a low heat for 15 minutes.
❦ Add the squash, cover and simmer for 20–25 minutes more until all the liquid has been absorbed. Serve immediately.

VARIATION: For Courgette, Rosemary and Lemon Rice, replace the herbs with 2 tablespoons of chopped fresh rosemary and 2 teaspoons of grated lemon zest. Replace the squash with 3 courgettes, quartered lengthways, and cut into chunks.

Lemon Rice with Mushrooms

SERVES 4

1 tbsp olive oil
75 g/3 oz butter
225 g/8 oz brown long-grain rice
450 ml/16 fl oz water
juice of 2 lemons
½ tsp salt

225 g/8 oz mixed wild or cultivated
  mushrooms (porcini, morels, ceps,
  chanterelles, flat cap), sliced
1 garlic clove, finely chopped
3 tbsp finely chopped fresh parsley
freshly ground black pepper

HEAT the oil and 25 g/1 oz of the butter in a pan. Add the rice and stir over a medium heat for 3 minutes, until transparent.

❧ Add the water, lemon juice and salt. Bring to the boil. Cover and simmer over a low heat for 40 minutes until all the liquid has been absorbed.

❧ Meanwhile, heat the remaining butter and stir-fry the mushrooms for 5 minutes. Add the garlic and fry until the liquid has evaporated.

❧ Fluff the rice with a fork, and stir in the mushrooms and parsley. Season to taste and serve.

Courgette Risotto

SERVES 4

350 g/12 oz courgettes, quartered
  lengthways and cut into chunks
3 tbsp olive oil
1 small onion, chopped
250 g/9 oz risotto rice

1 litre/1¾ pints boiling chicken stock,
  kept simmering
salt and freshly ground black pepper
25 g/1 oz butter
3 tbsp freshly grated Parmesan
  cheese

PUT the courgettes in a colander and sprinkle with salt. Leave to drain for 30 minutes, then pat dry.

❧ Heat 2 tablespoons of the oil in a pan, and fry the courgettes, cut side down, until slightly blackened. Remove from the pan.

❧ Heat the remaining oil, and gently fry the onion for 5 minutes.

❧ Add the rice, stirring until all the grains are coated with oil.

❧ Add a ladleful of the stock, and bring to the boil. Simmer until all the liquid has been absorbed. Continue until all the liquid has been absorbed and the rice is creamy.

❧ Stir in the courgettes, and season to taste.

❧ Remove from the heat, and quickly stir in the butter and cheese. Transfer to a warm serving dish and serve immediately.

Spinach Risotto

SERVES 4–6

1.2 kg/2¾ lb tender spinach,
  stalks removed
2 tbsp vegetable oil
40 g/1½ oz butter
1 small onion, finely chopped
250 g/9 oz risotto rice

¼ tsp grated nutmeg
salt and freshly ground black pepper
1 litre/1¾ pints boiling chicken stock,
  kept simmering
4 tbsp freshly grated Parmesan
  cheese

*P*LUNGE the spinach into plenty of boiling, salted water for 1 minute. Drain, squeeze dry thoroughly and chop.

❧ Heat the oil and 15 g/½ oz of butter in a large pan. Add the onion and gently fry until translucent.

❧ Add the rice and stir until the grains are coated and glossy. Stir in the spinach, nutmeg, and salt and pepper.

❧ Add a ladleful of stock, and stir over a low heat until the stock is absorbed. Continue stirring and adding stock, one ladle at a time, until the rice is tender but firm to bite. The mixture should be creamy but not runny.

❧ Stir in the Parmesan cheese and remaining butter, and serve immediately.

Golden Rice with Grilled Vegetables

SERVES 4–6

1 tbsp olive oil
225 g/8 oz long-grain brown rice
1 tsp ground turmeric
450 ml/16 fl oz stock
1 each red and yellow peppers,
  seeded and halved
3 small courgettes, halved lengthways

1 small aubergine, thickly sliced
  lengthways
2 small red onions, unpeeled and
  halved horizontally
olive oil, for brushing
3 tbsp chopped fresh coriander
salt and freshly ground black pepper

*H*EAT the oil in a saucepan, add the rice and turmeric, and stir until the grains are coated. Add the stock and bring to the boil. Stir once, cover and simmer over a very low heat for 40 minutes until the liquid has been absorbed.

❧ Meanwhile, brush the vegetables with oil. Place under a preheated hot grill for 10–15 minutes, turning and brushing with oil, until tender and beginning to blacken.

❧ Peel the onion and cut into chunks. Cut the remaining vegetables into chunks.

❧ Transfer the rice to a serving dish and top with the vegetables. Season to taste, sprinkle with coriander and drizzle over a little olive oil.

Mushroom Risotto

SERVES 4

75 g/3 oz butter
1 onion, sliced
225 g/8 oz medium-grain brown rice
150 ml/¼ pint dry white wine
600 ml/1 pint boiling stock, kept
  simmering

225 g/8 oz mushrooms, sliced
1 tbsp chopped fresh basil
salt and freshly ground black pepper
3 tbsp freshly grated Parmesan
  cheese

*M*ELT the butter in a saucepan, and fry the onion until golden. Stir in the rice, and cook for 5 minutes, stirring frequently.

❧ Add the wine, and bring to the boil. Continue boiling until well reduced. Stir in a ladleful of the stock, the mushrooms, basil and seasoning to taste. Simmer, stirring, until all the liquid has been absorbed.

❧ Continue gradually stirring in the stock until all the liquid has been absorbed.

❧ Stir in the Parmesan cheese, and serve immediately.

Aubergine and Egg Curry

SERVES 4–6

1 onion, finely chopped
6 tbsp vegetable oil
1 garlic clove, finely chopped
2 cm/¾ inch piece fresh ginger root
  finely chopped
1 fresh green chilli, seeded and finely
  chopped
½ tsp turmeric
2 tsp garam masala

1 aubergine, cubed
400 g/14 oz can chopped tomatoes
300 ml/½ pint stock
3 tbsp chopped fresh coriander
salt and freshly ground black pepper
4 hard-boiled eggs, halved
1 tbsp lemon juice
225 g/8 oz long-grain rice
coriander leaves, to garnish

*G*ENTLY fry the onion in the oil for 10 minutes. Add the garlic, ginger, chilli, turmeric, and garam masala, and fry for 5 minutes more. Add the aubergine and fry for 3 minutes.

❧ Stir in the tomatoes, stock, coriander and seasoning. Simmer gently, uncovered, for 30 minutes, adding a little water if the mixture becomes dry.

❧ Boil the rice in plenty of salted water until tender. Drain and keep warm.

❧ Meanwhile, carefully stir the eggs and lemon juice into the curry. Simmer for 10 minutes more.

❧ Serve on a bed of rice, garnished with coriander leaves.

Risotto alla Milanese

SERVES 4–6

2 tbsp olive oil
100 g/4 oz butter
1 small onion, finely chopped
450 g/1 lb risotto rice
½ tsp saffron, soaked in 3 tbsp
   hot water

150 ml/¼ pint dry white wine
1.5 litres/2½ pints boiling stock,
   kept simmering
salt and freshly ground black pepper
50 g/2 oz freshly grated Parmesan
   cheese

*H*EAT the oil with half the butter, and gently fry the onion for 3 minutes. Add the rice, and stir over a gentle heat for 5 minutes.

❧ Strain the saffron water into the rice. Add the wine, and cook briskly until well reduced.

❧ Add a ladleful of the stock to the rice, and cook until the liquid has been absorbed. Continue gradually adding the stock, until all the liquid has been absorbed. The rice should be creamy and not dry.

❧ Season to taste, stir in the remaining butter and the Parmesan cheese. Transfer to a warm serving dish and serve immediately.

Tomato and Olive Rice

SERVES 4

1 tbsp vegetable oil
1 onion, chopped
1 garlic clove, crushed
225 g/8 oz long-grain rice
6 tomatoes, peeled and quartered
300 ml/½ pint stock

salt and freshly ground black pepper
finely grated zest of ½ lemon
2 tsp finely chopped fresh rosemary
50 g/2 oz black olives, pitted and
   sliced
lemon wedges, to garnish

*H*EAT the oil in a saucepan, and gently fry the onion and garlic for 3 minutes. Add the rice, and fry for 5 minutes.

❧ Add the tomatoes, stock, seasoning, lemon zest and rosemary. Bring to the boil, cover and simmer for 15–20 minutes until the rice is tender and the liquid has been absorbed.

❧ Stir in the olives, and adjust the seasoning if necessary. Transfer to a warm serving dish, garnish with the lemon wedges and serve immediately.